DATE DUE

PRINTED IN U.S.A.

My
Respiratory
System
A 4D Book

by Martha E. H. Rustad

Consultant:
Natasha Kasbekar, M.D., Pediatrician
Kids Health Partners, LLC, Skokie, Ill.

PEBBLE
a capstone imprint

Download the Capstone 4D app!

- Ask an adult to download the Capstone 4D app.
- Scan the cover and stars inside the book for additional content.

When you scan a spread, you'll find fun extra stuff to go with this book! You can also find these things on the web at www.capstone4D.com using the password: breath.00214

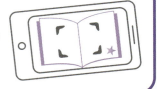

Pebble Plus is published by Pebble
1710 Roe Crest Drive, North Mankato, Minnesota 56003
www.mycapstone.com

Library of Congress Cataloging-in-Publication Data
Names: Rustad, Martha E. H. (Martha Elizabeth Hillman), 1975– author.
Title: My respiratory system : a 4D book / by Martha E. H. Rustad.
Description: North Mankato, Minnesota : Pebble, a Capstone imprint,
    [2019] | Series: Pebble plus. My body systems | Audience: Ages 4–8.
Identifiers: LCCN 2018004145 (print) | LCCN 2018005882 (ebook) |
    ISBN 9781977100290 (eBook PDF) | ISBN 9781977100214 (hardcover) |
    ISBN 9781977100252 (pbk.)
Subjects: LCSH: Respiratory organs—Juvenile literature. | Respiration—
    Juvenile literature. | Lungs—Juvenile literature.
Classification: LCC QP121 (ebook) | LCC QP121 .R855 2019 (print) |
    DDC 612.2—dc23
LC record available at https://lccn.loc.gov/2018004145

Editorial Credits
Emily Raij, editor; Charmaine Whitman, designer; Morgan Walters,
media researcher; Laura Manthe, production specialist

Image Credits
iStockphoto: FatCamera, 15; Shutterstock: Africa Studio, (boy) Cover,
1, Alex Mit, (inset) Cover, 13, eveleen, 11, Maria Averburg, (clouds)
design element, Medical Art Inc, 9, Rawpixel.com, 20, Seika Chujo, 7,
supparsorn, 19, Tetiana Saienko, (lungs) Cover, wavebreakmedia, 5,
Zurijeta, 17

Note to Parents and Teachers

The My Body Systems set supports the national science standards related to structures and processes. This book describes and illustrates the respiratory system. The images support early readers in understanding the text. The repetition of words and phrases helps early readers learn new words. This book also introduces early readers to subject-specific vocabulary words, which are defined in the Glossary section. Early readers may need assistance to read some words and to use the Table of Contents, Glossary, Read More, Internet Sites, Critical Thinking Questions, and Index sections of the book.

Printed and bound in the United States.
PA017

Table of Contents

Breath and Lungs

It's my birthday!

I blow out my candles.

I use my breath.

My breath is made of air.

Let's follow my breath.

I use my respiratory system
to breathe. It starts with
my nose or mouth. A place
behind my nose warms, wets,
and cleans the air.

The air goes down my trachea.

This tube starts in my throat.

Then it splits into two tubes.

The tubes send air to my lungs.

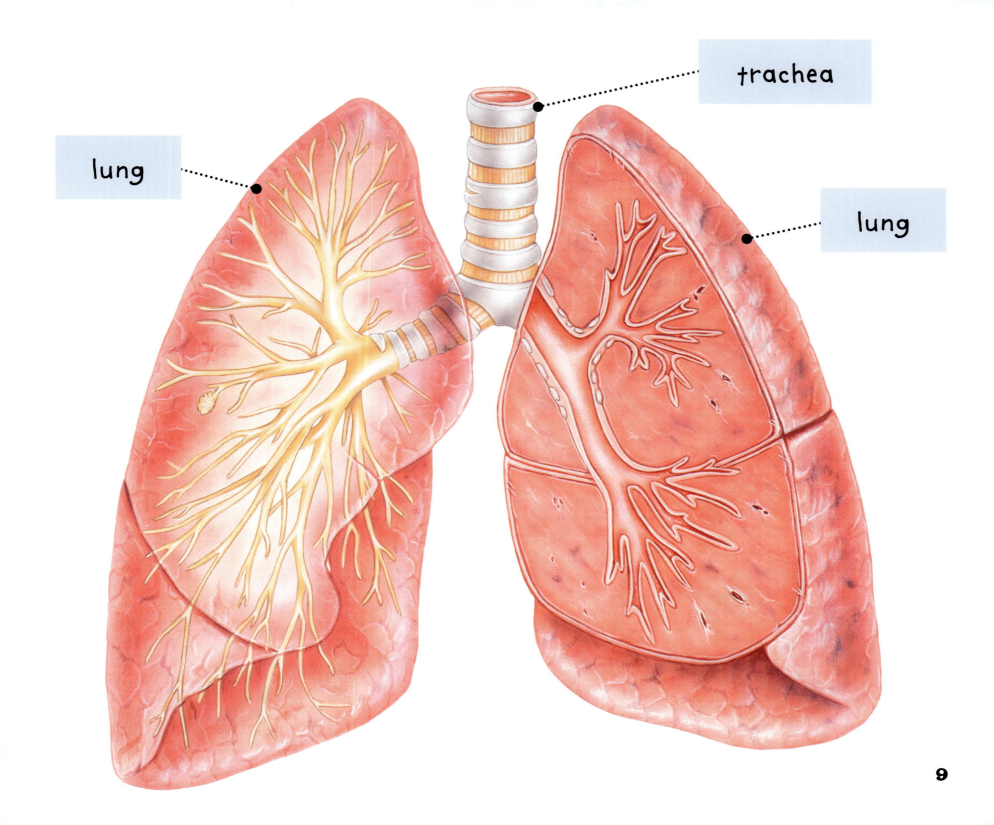

trachea

lung

lung

9

My diaphragm is a muscle.

It helps me take in air.

I breathe in. My diaphragm

makes space for my lungs

to fill up.

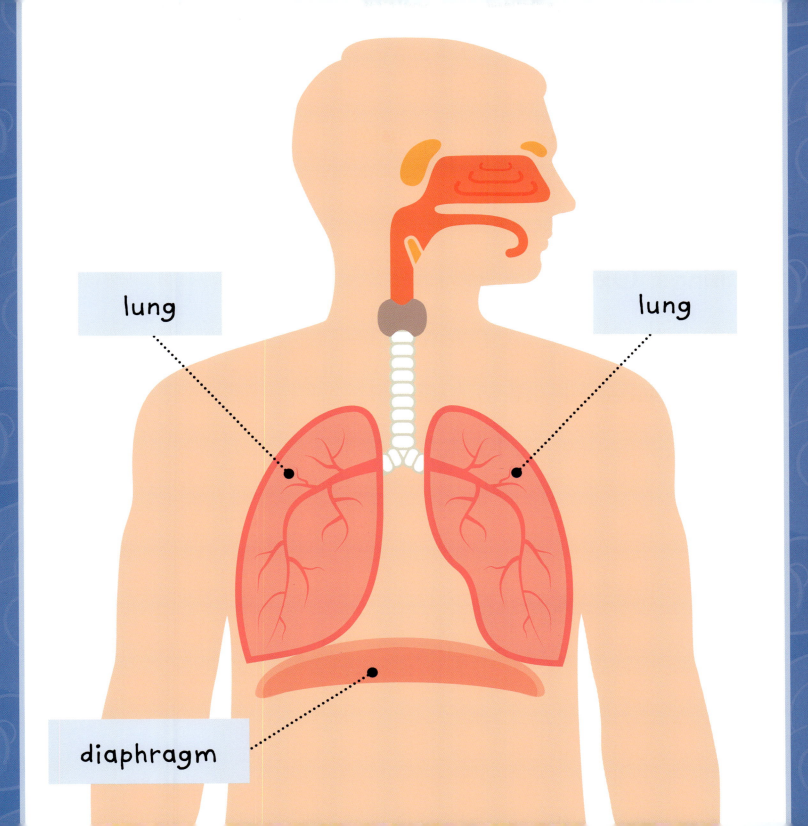

lung

lung

diaphragm

Oxygen and Carbon Dioxide

Alveoli are air sacs in my lungs. Oxygen passes through the alveoli. It goes into my blood vessels. Blood vessels carry oxygen to my body.

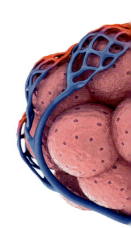

oxygen

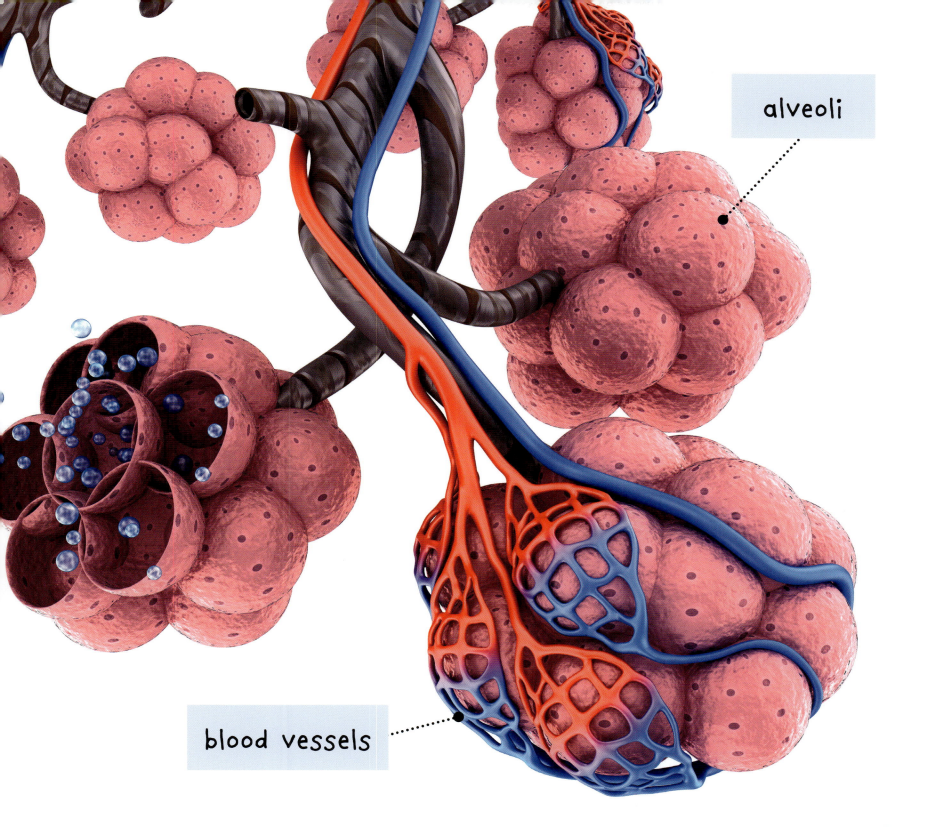

alveoli

blood vessels

Oxygen is a gas in the air.
Food and oxygen mix in
my body. This makes energy.
Energy keeps my whole
body working.

My lungs help my body
remove waste. Carbon dioxide
is a gas. It is also waste
in the body. I breathe it out.

Keeping Lungs Healthy

I help my lungs so they can help me. Washing my hands keeps germs away.
I stay away from smoke and dirty air too.

I exercise to keep my lungs healthy. Exercise makes my lungs stronger. Stronger lungs make it easier to breathe. Bodies need to breathe!

Glossary

alveoli—little air sacs inside your lungs where blood picks up oxygen

blood vessel—a narrow tube that carries blood through your body

carbon dioxide—a colorless, odorless gas made by the act of breathing

diaphragm—the muscle under your lungs that moves as you breathe

energy—the strength to do active things without getting tired

germ—a tiny living thing that causes sickness

muscle—a tissue in the body that is made of strong fibers; muscles can be tightened or relaxed to make the body move.

oxygen—a colorless gas that people and animals breathe; humans and animals need oxygen to live.

respiratory—related to the process of breathing

sac—a small pocket or bag

trachea—the air passage that connects the nose and the mouth to the lungs

Read More

Brett, Flora. *Your Respiratory System Works!* Your Body Systems. North Mankato, Minn.: Capstone Press, 2015.

Figorito, Christine. *The Lungs in Your Body.* Let's Find Out! The Human Body. New York: Britannica Educational Publishing, in association with Rosen Educational Services, 2015.

Kenney, Karen Latchana. *Respiratory System.* Amazing Body Systems. Minneapolis: Jump!, Inc., 2017.

Internet Sites

Use FactHound to find Internet sites related to this book.

Visit *www.facthound.com*

Just type in 9781977100214 and go.

Super-cool stuff! Check out projects, games and lots more at **www.capstonekids.com**

Critical Thinking Questions

1. How can you keep your lungs healthy?

2. What carries oxygen to your body? Why do you need oxygen?

3. What do you breathe out?

Index